You Fill Up My Senses

Meditations on Solomon's Full Sensory Love Song

By

Rev. James DuJack

Printed in the United States of America

First Printing, 2013

ISBN-13: 9780615675237
ISBN- 10:0615675239

Oakwood Covenant Press
260 Oakwood Avenue
Troy, NY 12182

DEDICATION

To my father and my mother, who gave
me life and made it full.
From dad comes the inclination to
analyze; from mom, the inclination to
appreciate! My thoughts and thanks are
toward you both!

Presented in celebration of their 60th
Wedding Anniversary.

PREFACE

"You Fill Up My Senses"! Perhaps you remember those words as the opening and repeating lyrics in John Denver's "Annie's Song". Whatever certain symbolic aspects there are pointing to Christ and His Church, at root, the Song of Solomon is about the most intimate love between a man and a woman. The more we understand and apply Solomon, the fuller our lives will be, with fading and fewer shades of gray.

CONTENTS

Each chapter represents the notes which formed a series of sermons delivered to Oakwood Bible Church. Hence the reader will find references throughout to the saints and situations at Oakwood.

CHAPTER 1:
THE SPARK OF LOVE

Song of Solomon 1:1 "The Song of songs, which is Solomon's. Let him kiss me with the kisses of his mouth: for thy love is better than wine."

The Spark of Love: it is perhaps among the most famous paintings of all, rivaled only by some of his other works as well as those of DaVinci. At the Vatican, St. Peter's square in Rome, high atop the ceiling of the Sistine Chapel, there is one of Michelangelo's greatest works, the 1511 *"The Creation of Adam"*. There we see the outstretched hand and index finger of God, tantalizingly close to the equally outstretched hand and index finger of Adam.

God's right arm is outstretched to impart the **Spark of Life:** contact, touch, connection, and transference. Perhaps, you might call this a *Covenant Encounter*. The Spark of Life being infused into man is the stuff of Genesis 2. It is wonderful and meaningful, this Spark of Life, being far superior to our thoughts of "Touched by an Angel" or "ET Phone Home".

The Song of Solomon is about the **Spark of Love**. Here, fleshed out before us in so many ways, is the power, the energy, and the **Spark of Love** that comes from God. Of course, we can know it on a human level, and that human level is depicted for us here in this Book.

On a human level, love is meaningful, it is exhilarating, and it changes everything. How much more then is the pure and exquisite delight of those that love and are loved by God.

The theme of the Song of Solomon is **The Beloved:**

1

those loved by God with the same love which He has for His Son. "**The Beloved**" is mentioned as such in every chapter, except Chapter Three, where he is referred to as "**him who my soul loveth**".

*Song of Solomon 3:1 "By night on my bed I sought **him whom my soul loveth:** I sought him, but I found him not."*

*Song of Solomon 3:4 "It was but a little that I passed from them, but I found **him whom my soul loveth:** I held him, and would not let him go, until I had brought him into my mother's house, and into the chamber of her that conceived me."*

Beloved is mentioned some thirty times throughout the book of the Song of Solomon. Look at just the last one.

Song of Solomon 8:14 "Make haste, my beloved, and be thou like to a roe or to a young hart upon the mountains of spices".

Beloved at Oakwood: you are referred to in the New Testament, some fifty-five times as **The Beloved**. We are the Agapetos, **The Beloved**. A friend at Seminary had a license plate that said "Agapetos". Biblical writers, Peter, Paul, James John, and Jude, all refer to God's people as **The Beloved**.

Brethren, we, like Adam are the recipients of a Covenant Encounter, and not just the **Spark of Life,** but the **Spark of Love** is ours as well. One Jewish Rabbi refers to the Song of Solomon as the "Holy of Holies". Remember the Tabernacle; it was all about access, all about access and proximity: outside the camp, in the camp, approaching God, curtains, gates, court yards, altar, lavel, Holy Place, then the Most Holy Place.

This book, the Song of Solomon: it is intimacy, it is

fellowship, it is union with God. The Song of Solomon is read by the Jews at Passover, the feast we now celebrate in Communion. Everything about this book, on both a human and spiritual level, is better felt than telt. Nonetheless, I will do my best to communicate some of this Covenant Encounter, the literary depiction of the Spark of Love.

This literary depiction of the Spark of Love will take us on a journey, in which all of the senses will be addressed. The Song of Solomon is sensuous in the purest meaning of the word; (touch, taste, smell, sight, and sound).

The Beloved knows and is known, and the Biblical sense of the word "to know" is sexual. This Covenant involves parties that have both names and bodies. The Song of Solomon is not often preached in protestant circles because in our gnosticism we love ideas about God more than we love God.

Let me quickly preview some of the ground we are going to cover. I read to you, verse 1, simply a title.

Song of Solomon 1:1-2 "The song of songs, which is Solomon's. Let him kiss me with the kisses of his mouth: for thy love is better than wine."

In the Hebrew, the first word of the song is **(yissaqeni) "kiss me"**. Talk about contact, talk about intimacy, this would make Michelangelo **blush**. This is not the **Spark of Life**; this is the **Spark of Love**. **"Kiss me"** is a direct, passionate appeal for intimacy. "This person doesn't want to talk theology, get on a committee, study apologetics or do church work".[1] Do we hear this

---

[1] A masterpiece of Pastoral insight; "Five Smooth Stones for

in each other? With and to God and each other, life is to be joined, intimacy makes us whole.   Verbalized or not, the cry of every heart is **"kiss me"**.   Supporting this request is this rationale: why do we want to be kissed, because love is better than wine.   Wine is good in the Bible; it's festive and represents feasting.   Feasting is not a solitary act or event.   Feasting requires and demands intimacy, some level of community.   Wine is festive, and it lasts a while, but love is better.

We are not yet to the third verse, and already we've seen kiss me and wine. This is sure to be a best seller, but wait, there's more, a lot more. Let's look at verse three.

Song of Solomon 1:3 "Because of thy savour of thy good ointments thy name is an ointment poured forth, therefore do the virgins love thee".

Here we have fragrance, perfume, and cologne.   A month ago, I preached on making scents of Christmas. I haven't gotten that sermon out of my mind and heart. Our relationship with God reflects our relationships on earth and is to be a full sensory experience.

*Malachi 1:11 For from the rising of the sun even unto the going down of the same my name shall be great among the Gentiles; and in every place **incense** shall be offered unto my name, and a pure offering: for my name shall be great among the heathen, saith the Lord of Hosts."*

We will find incense and perfume all over The Song of Songs! Maybe not familiar brands such as Charlie, Channell, Estee Lauder, or even Love Potion #9. Ah,

---

Pastoral Work" by Eugene Petersen, p. 43ff. informs this and several other thematic issues throughout this series.

but wait, the perfume, as good as it is, only prepares the way for an even greater sensory pleasure. "Your name is an oil poured out": I love the sound of your name. I love to hear it. I love to say it. I love to speak it. I love to sing it.

This is a person in love. The name represents the persons very being. People have names; people are not machines or numbers. There are names all over the Bible. Jesus used and uses names; he said "Peter"; he said "Mary"; he said "Lazarus, come forth"! God is not here addressing, "You People". He's addressing Allen, Karen, Chuck, Gary, Norma, Michael, Kristan, and Erin. Ah, this book: kiss me, wine, perfume, names.

Over in chapter 2, we will deal with sounds, the voice of my beloved. Your voice is a barometer. It is expressing; "it is wonderful to hear your voice", or "I can't stand to hear the sound of your voice".

In chapters 3, 4, and 5, we will explore, The Beloved has a body, a body embraced. It is looked upon, felt, tasted, and delighted in. It is a body needing to be found, seen, talked to, and touched.

These sparks of love also contain other elements, elements found in all relationships. All over the book, but particularly in chapters 5-8, we see things like expectation, fears, and abandonment. There is loneliness represented in chapter 5:6, and disappointment along with pain in chapter 5:2-5. Chapter 1:6 shows vulnerability and insecurity; she is sun scorched, not nicely tanned. There is quite an emphasis on how well endowed the lovers are. There is also the risk of exposing one's self, sexually and in every other way (chapter 6:5). A flock of goats is a good thing! So is a flock of sheep, which goes up from the

5

washing. (Chapter 6:6)

We will talk so much about the body. Our bodies are the medium through which we do everything. They are the medium through which we dance before God and with God.

The Song of Solomon is not the only book in the Bible where we find sexual intimacy. As we look through it further, we will contrast it with the several other books in the Bible where sexual intimacy is used to depict man's unfaithfulness to God, his perversion, his treachery, and lastly, his adultery.

This Song of Solomon depicts the full sensory delight of a faithful love relationship. Sparks will fly and they will be sparks of Love all given in this Song of Songs.

Song of Solomon 1:1 "The Song of songs, which is Solomon's. Let him kiss me with the kisses of his mouth: for thy love is better than wine."

Do not diminish God's contact. His provision is the application of oil to make you whole.

CHAPTER 2:
THE POWER OF TOUCH

Song of Solomon 1:1 – 2a "The Song of songs, which is Solomon's. Let him kiss me with the kisses of his mouth: for thy love is better than wine. Let him kiss me with the kisses of his mouth."

In the previous chapter, I presented an overview of the Song of Solomon. I made note of the magnificent painting by Michelangelo, high atop in the ceiling of the Sistine chapel, located at the Vatican's St Peters square in Rome, Italy. There we see the 1511 masterpiece called *"The Creation of Adam"*. There we see the outstretched hand and index finger of God, tantalizingly, yet so close to the equally outstretched hand and index finger of Adam.

This is a covenant encounter, a pictorial of the truth of Genesis 2. There is contact, touch, connection, and transfer. We previously talked about the **Spark of Love**; we will now explore the **Power of Touch**.

The Song of Solomon is a "full sensory" expression of a love relationship between a man and his wife, and by extension the love relationship between Christ and His Church. A full sensory expression includes, **sight, sound, smell, taste, and touch**. Each of these is found in abundance in the Song of Solomon: our love for God, and love for each other, their love for us, and God's love for us involves all these things.

Gnostics may be satisfied in loving ideas. Christians love God and other persons in and with full sensory expressions. "The Beloved" is the theme of this book, and is referred to some thirty times therein. Christians are

7

referred to as "The Beloved" some fifty-five times in the New Testament.

All the stuff we find and see about marriage in the Bible is also a microcosmic picture of the marriage of Jesus and His bride, the Church.

Ephesians 5:22-33 "Wives, submit yourselves unto your own husbands, as unto the Lord. For the husband is the head of the wife, even as Christi is the head of the church: and he is the savior of the body. Therefore, as the church is subject unto Christ, so let the wives be to their own husbands in everything. Husbands love your wives, even as Christ also loved the church, and gave himself for it. That he might sanctify and cleanse it with the washing of water by the word. That he might present it to himself a glorious church, not having spot, or wrinkle, or any such thing, but that it should be hold and without blemish. So ought men to love their wives as their own bodies. He that loveth his wife loveth himself. For no man ever yet hated his own flesh; but nourisheth and cherisheth it, even as the Lord the church. For we are members of his body, of his flesh and of his bones. For this cause shall a man leave his father and mother, and shall be joined unto his wife and they two shall be one flesh. This is a great mystery: but I speak concerning Christ and the church. Nevertheless let every one of you in particular so love his wife even as himself; and the wife see that she reverence her husband."

Everything we see in the Song: touch, taste, sight, sound, smell, all of it, is about our relationship with God and is made possible by **Jesus Christ**.

Ephesians 2:18 "For through him we both have access by one Spirit unto the Father."

As we explore this **full sensory** relationship, it is all and only made possible by the mercy and merit of Jesus Christ. As I previously mentioned, one Rabbi refers to the Song of Solomon as the **"Holy of Holies"**. Let me say that again, the Song of Solomon is the **"Holy of Holies"**. What an astoundingly insightful comment!

Remember the tabernacle. It was all about access, all about access and proximity; about who gets in and how to get in. If you are outside the camp, you are wondering how do I get in to the camp, who and how does one approach God. There are the curtains, the gates, the courtyard, the alter, the laver, the Holy Place, then the **Most Holy place**, and finally the **Holy of Holies**.

This book is about contact, intimacy, fellowship and through Jesus Christ, union. It is full sensory; as every marriage should be, and it begins with **touch**.[2] The **cry** "Kiss Me" is a verbal touch, a verbal connection. The first word of the book in Hebrew is: **Yissaqeni.**

"Kiss Me"; this is a direct passionate appeal for intimacy and what a rebuke to the **gnostic and intellectual, modern Church.** This person doesn't want to memorize the catechism or a spot on a governing board. This person wants a touch and contact with God!

A kiss is a touch, an intimate one. It is not necessarily a sexual issue. It is too bad that in our depraved culture the words kiss and touch have almost always an exclusively sexual overtone.

Kiss and touch are for intimacy, and in a kiss and touch, there is great power. We won't look at all the instances of touching here in the Song, but it is

---

[2] For a fabulous presentation on the power and importance of touch, see a correspondence written by Rev. Richard Bledsoe, reproduced in James Jordan's "The Handwriting on the Wall". P. 536-537

throughout, and it not only opens with touch, it closes with touch as well.

Song of Solomon 2:6 "His left hand is under my head and his right hand doth embrace me."

Song of Solomon 8:3 "His left hand should be under my head, and his right hand should embrace me".

"Song of Solomon 8:5a "Who is this that cometh up from the wilderness, leaning upon her beloved?"

"Leaning"; this contact empowers through the most difficult times. This is a picture of support and of sin transfer. Leaning is the beginning sacrificial work in Leviticus. We lean on Jesus and begin our walk into the promised land. The revelation and use of touch to strengthen, to empower, and to heal is throughout the Bible.

Let us look at just a few:

1 Kings 19:5 "And as he lay and slept under a juniper tree, behold, then an angel touched him, and said unto him, arise and eat".

Isaiah 6:7 "And he laid it upon my mouth, and said Lo, this hath touched thy lips; and thine iniquity is taken away, and thy sin purged".

Daniel 8:18 "Now as he was speaking with me, I was in a deep sleep on my face toward the ground; and he touched me, and set me upright".

Daniel 10:10 "And behold, a hand touched me, which set me upon my knees and upon the palms of my hands".

Daniel 10:16 "And behold, one like the similitude of the sons of men touched my lips; then I opened my mouth and spake, and said unto him that stood before me, O my Lord, by the vision my sorrows are turned upon me and I have retained no strength."

Daniel 10:18 " Then there came again and touched me one like the appearance of a man, and he strengthened me."

Touch brings strength, power, healing, and comfort. Let us not forget the comfort in Psalm 139.

Psalm 139:5 "Thou has beset me behind and before, and laid thine hand upon me".

Psalm 139:10 "Even there shall thy hand lead me, and they right hand shall hold me."

In Psalm 23:4, even the rod and staff bring comfort.

Psalm 23:4 "Yeah though I walk through the valley of the shadow of death, I will fear no evil; for thou art with me; thy rod and thy staff they comfort me".

We see this all the more with Jesus in the New Testament. Of course, he could "speak the word only and people would be healed", but we are humans and so he also touches. It is all over the Gospels, let's look at a handful.

Matthew 8:8 "the centurion answered and said, Lord, I am not worthy that thou shouldest come under my roof; but speak the word only and my servant shall be healed".

Matthew 8:14-15 "And when Jesus was come into Peter's house, he saw his wife's mother laid, and sick of a fever. And he touched her hand, and the fever left her; and she arose, and ministered unto them."

11

We see in Matthew 14:31, when St. Peter was sinking, that Jesus stretched forth his **hand and caught him.**

Matthew 14:31 "And immediately Jesus stretched forth his hand, and caught him, and said unto him, O thou of little faith, wherefore didst thou doubt?"

In Luke 5:13, we find a leper that was healed and restored to human contact, even though we are told **don't touch lepers.**

Luke 5:13 "And he put forth his hand, and touched him, saying, I will; be thou clean. And immediately the leprosy departed from him."

In Luke 7:14, we find someone dead, brought back to life and restored to human contact, even though we are told **don't touch the dead.**

Luke 7:14 "And he came touched the bier; and they that bare him stood still. And he said, young man, I say unto thee, Arise."

Over in Luke 22:50 – 51, we see Jesus not only healing an enemy but also **touching** him.

Luke 22:50-51 "And one of them smote the servant of the high priest, and cut off his right ear. And Jesus answered and said, suffer ye thus far. And he touched his ear, and healed him."

The "kiss me" of the Song of Solomon is the cry of every human heart, the cry for love, intimacy, contact and for touch. Let me repeat, it's not all exclusively sexual. Are you ready?

Romans 16:16 "Salute one another with a holy kiss, the churches of Christ salute you."

1 Corinthians 16:20 "All the brethren greet you, greet ye one another with a holy kiss".

2 Corinthians 13:12 "Greet one another with an holy kiss."

1 Thessalonians 5:26 "Greet all the brethren with an holy kiss."

1 Peter 5:14a "Greet ye one another with a kiss of charity."

Kissing is not always exclusively sexual, but it is, and it demands intimacy.

The "kiss me" of the Song of Solomon is a direct, passionate appeal for intimacy, for contact, for touch. When those two young girls, Audrey and Lilly were baptized, in some sense through the symbol of water, God was touching, contacting them, marking them, purifying them, making them like Esther.

God is not opposed to touch; only in our depraved perversity has touch become such a taboo. One of the most interesting, helpful and practical books I have read is "The Five Love Languages".[3] The five love languages are as follows:

Words of Affirmation
Quality Time
Acts of Service
Gifts
Physical Touch

I've seen this played out in all my relationships,

---

[3] Written by Gary Chapman; this book challenges the contemporary wisdom and tract toward "making sure you treat people the same".

including my dogs. Teddy is a contact dog, a leaner; he sits on your foot. Ketty needs sweet talk.

I can remember from way back, I think it was in 1995 at our school, at a teachers orientation; we showed a video of teachers as models and examples.[4] One of the adults interviewed, recounted how, as a youngster in class, "the teacher would go around the room and then she put her hand on my shoulder, and **I hated it**". Right after stating; "and I hated it", there was a pause and the person said; "**and I loved it**". That person themselves, went on to be a teacher!

In 1969, a rock band called "The Who"; perhaps you are inquiring: "The Who"? That's right "The Who", put out a block buster album titled "Tommy". Now, unquestionably the 60's and The Who had perverse elements, nonetheless, not seeing, hearing, or speaking, his theme song lyrics include these:

*See me, feel me, **touch me**; heal me.*

Tommy was a blind, deaf, and dumb boy who went on to become, (of all things) a pin-ball wizard.

Brothers and sisters, every relationship you have can be enhanced if it is full sensory, and good relationships help us enormously to be healthy. Sure, there is danger in full sensory relationships, but all true love is dangerous. Made in the image of God, we are the body of Christ and love is a contact sport.

"That which was from the beginning, which we have heard, which we have seen with our eyes, which we have looked upon, and our

---

[4] "Molder of Dreams" as I recall.

hands have handled, of the Word of Life." 1 John 1:1

Jesus has dealt in an incarnational way with us, and we are to deal in an incarnational way with each other. Through Jesus Christ, we have access to the Holy of Holies. Make no mistake about the awesome power of touch!

A special form of touch is a kiss. Next up "Let Him kiss me with the kisses of His mouth" *Song of Solomon 1:2*.

CHAPTER 3:
SOLOMON'S KISS AND TELL

"The Song of songs, which is Solomon's. Let him kiss me with the kisses of his mouth; for thy love is better than wine. Because of the savour of thy good ointments thy name is as ointment poured forth, therefore do the virgins love thee. Draw me, we will run after thee; the king hath brought me into his chambers: we will be glad and rejoice in thee, we will remember thy love more than wine: the upright love thee. I am black, but comely, O ye daughters of Jerusalem, as the tents of Kedar, as the curtains of Solomon. Look not upon me, because I am black, because the sun hath looked upon me: my mother's children were angry with me; they make me the keeper of the vineyards; but my own vineyard have I not kept. Tell me, O thou whom my soul loveth, where thou feedest, where thou makest thy flock to rest at noon: for why should I be as one that turneth aside by the flocks of thy companions." Song of Solomon 1:1-7

This morning we are continuing our study of the Song of Solomon, recognizing that it represents a Full Sensory Expression of a love relationship. Last time we talked about the Power of Touch. In this chapter we will explore Sound; specifically verbal communication.

Our passage begins with "Kiss Me"; a kiss is a type of touch, but "Kiss Me" is also a cry. A cry out for attention. As we have noted, this is a direct, passionate appeal for intimacy.

How important are words, how important is talk? Well, first, for some people words are their love language. Remember we talked about those five love languages; quality time, acts of service, gifts, physical touch and words of encouragement or words of affirmation.

For some, even a whisper, even the whisper of a sweet

something; for some, even the whisper of sweet nothings into a loved one's ear can make all the difference. Of course, love languages can be used for and by manipulative motivations, but if we truly aim to love, we must learn and apply love languages. Words are one of these languages, and a powerful one.

Let me recount the classic stereotype. A man and his wife of forty years are now in counseling. They have everything, material success of every sort. They are nice neighbors, with grown, healthy, and respectable children. The husband in many respects is a great provider, and protector. Physical touch was abundant, no problem at all, but the wife was starved for conversation. She tells the counselor, "He never talks to me" and "I can't tell you the last time he told me, he loved me". The husband interrupts, "Look I told you I love you. On our wedding night I told you that I love you, if anything changes, I will let you know."

Valentine's Day may have come and gone. Some may be breathing a sigh of relief, but for many others, we still just don't get it. Now this is not just a gender or romantic issue, all of us, as we are commanded to love, must recognize the **value of words**.

Last week we saw how many letters to the early church closed with the charge that they greet and salute each other with a holy kiss, a touch. Today, we simply note that those letters were written, written to be read, written to be read aloud, and **written to be heard**.

Christians are "people of the book". Ours is a religion of the **ear**: faith comes by hearing. God is the Word, and the Word is to be heard.

We've referenced and made note that one Rabbi calls

the Song of Solomon, the Holy of Holies, that place of full sensory access, intimacy, union with God. Full sensory, Touch and Words: this is the Song of Songs. It is the best of the best of verbal communication. We could view it as the chant of Solomon, as song and chant means the same thing as canticles.

God is a great revealer, the great communicator. Don't ever doubt the power of words.

Genesis 1:1-3 "In the beginning God created the heaven and the earth. And the earth was without form, and void; and darkness was upon the face of the deep. And the spirit of God moved upon the face of the waters. And God said, let there be light: and there was light."

Psalm 29:3-9 "The voice of the LORD is upon the waters: the God of glory thundereth: the LORD is upon many waters. The voice of the LORD is powerful; the voice of the LORD is full of majesty. The voice of the LORD breaketh the cedars; yea, the LORD breaketh the cedars of Lebanon. He maketh them also to skip like a calf; Lebanon and Sirion like a young unicorn. The voice of the LORD shaketh the wilderness; the LORD shaketh the wilderness of Kadesh. The voice of the LORD maketh the hinds to calve, and discovereth the forests: and in his temple doeth every one speak of his glory." The voice of the Lord is full and perfect: seven times.

Psalm 68:11 "The Lord gave the word: great was the company of those that published it." The voice of the Lord is published and proclaimed.

Psalm 118:14 "The LORD is my strength and song, and is become my salvation". God is our Song and Salvation.

The Gospel reading opens with the Word. John 1:1-14. In verse 18, Jesus declares Himself to be the exegete, that is the **expression** of God.

1 John 1:1 also highlights the Word.

Pastor Jason has been in Hebrews;
Hebrews 1:1 spoke;
Hebrews 1:2 spoken
Hebrews 1:3 power of Word.

James 3 is all about the power of the tongue.
James 3:1-13
Power to direct (ships and people)
Power to destroy
Power to delight

God is a great communicator with His bride.
Jeremiah 33:3 "Call unto me and I will answer thee, and show thee great and might things, which thou knowest not". Likewise, there is much talk between the beloveds in the Song of Solomon 2:10 "My beloved spake, and said unto me, Rise up, my love, my fair one, and come away." I need not remind you that we are the Beloved, designated as such some fifty-five times in the New Testament. The Beloveds in the Song of Solomon are constantly talking with each other with affirming words. The "Content" of their words will impact us further when we discuss sight and smell, but the fact is they continuously affirm each other in conversation.

You look great! You smell fantastic! And they both **"said so"**; "telling each other". Let's see this together.

Song of Solomon 1:15-16 "Behold, thou art fair, my love; behold, thou art fair; thou has doves' eyes. Behold, thou art fair, my beloved, yea, pleasant: also our bed is green."
Song of Solomon 4:1, "Behold thou art fair, my love; behold, thou art fair; thou hast doves' eyes within thy locks: thy hair is as a flock of goats, that appear from mount Gilead.

20

Song of Solomon 4:7 "Thou art all fair, my love; there is no spot in thee."

In the movie, "Gods and Generals" General Jackson and his wife are sweet, courteous, polite, and respectful.

Song of Solomon 7:9 "And the roof of thy mouth like the best wine for my beloved, that goeth down sweetly, causing the lips of those that are asleep to speak." They loved each other so much that they talked in their sleep.

By the way if you ever wondered why females have a thing with shoes, it's Biblical, look at *Song of Solomon 7:1a "How beautiful are thy feet with shoes."*

Song of Solomon 5:2 "I sleep, but my heart waketh: it is the voice of my beloved that knocketh, saying Open to me, my sister, my love, my dove, my undefiled: for my head is filled with dew, and my locks with the drops of night." They dream about each other, they hear each other in their dreams. The voice is so powerful, and it is a powerful barometer of the relationship.

Song of Solomon 2:8 "The voice of my beloved! Behold, he cometh leaping upon the mountains, skipping upon the hills." The voice of my beloved, for some, the voice of the other is not a dream but more of a nightmare. I've mentioned this before in counseling, the voice is a barometer both in my own experience and as a counselor. "It is so wonderful to hear your voice" (8000 miles away). "I can't stand to hear the sound of his voice" (8 millimeters away). The relationship described here in the Song of Solomon is not a nightmare but indeed dreamlike.

I titled this "Solomon's Kiss and Tell". I did so because of *Song of Solomon 1:7 "Tell me, O thou whom my soul loveth, where thou feedest, where thou makest thy flock to rest at noon: for why should I be as one that turneth aside by the flocks of thy companions?"* This is a great verse! It is very revealing and instructive; verse two mentions a kiss; verse seven mentions to tell. Her desire for verbal contact is as strong as her desire for physical contact. The book starts "kiss me" and verse seven says "tell me". She wants to know. Now the skeptics and cynical among us might conclude, yup, this sound a lot like nagging, smothering nagging. Tell me, where are you at breakfast. Tell me, where are you at noon. She wants to know, her world is wound up in his world. Note, she is not trying to get him to change his work or stop working, or question his calling, none of that. She wants to know. It is not nagging, she just needs some reassurance.

In verse eight he invites her to tag along with sweet loving words. Her cry "kiss me" and "tell me" are both all about the desire for intimacy. She wants to be loved, to be touched, and to be talked to!

In *Song of Solomon 1:7b "for why should I be as one that turneth aside by the flocks of thy companions".* She wants to be special. Not just another plain Jane or as the language alludes to here, a prostitute.

As Christians, we often need re-assurance. That is why God gives us His Word. *"Call unto me and I will answer thee."* This morning, I want to close with a greater Solomon's kiss and tell. Jesus has left us with the edible and the audible Word. He has spoken to us, and He feeds us. As we close today let us consider: His love for us, our love for Him, and the love we are to have one for another.

Song of Solomon 8:13 "Thou that dwellest in the gardens, the companions hearken to thy voice: cause me to hear it.

We who by Jesus Christ dwell in access to the Holy of

22

Holies; let us remember that love involves and includes both **kiss** and **tell**, and as we tell, as we speak, may God grant us the power and cause us to hear the joyful sound, that Jesus saves.

CHAPTER 4:
SOLOMON'S FEAST

Song of Solomon 2:4 "He brought me to the banqueting house, and his banner over me was love".

Solomon's Feast: Let us explore it thematically, as a full sensory expression of a love relationship. God is not a gnostic. We are not to be gnostics.

The Song of Solomon has been called the "Holy of Holies". That place of full sensory intimacy, communion, and yes even union with God. All the walls, coverings, and obstacles are removed. We have full access through our Lord Jesus Christ. Do not lose sight of that, God is not accessible any other way. This full sensory access includes sight, sound, smell, touch, and taste.

Thus far, we have looked at the power of touch. Touching is all over the Song of Solomon as it is over all full sensory love relationships.

Also, we looked at Solomon's kiss and tell. There we talked about the need for verbal communication and affirmation. Affirming words, like physical touch, are well known love languages. I think it was Mark Twain who once said, "I can live for two months on a good compliment."

Last time out, we focused on 1:7; "**Tell Me**"; It was "**Solomon's Kiss & Tell**"; verse 2 said "**Kiss Me**". The need to be talked to was as great as the need to be touched. As a matter of fact, this need and desire to be talked to was as important, that without talk, the bride was reduced to feeling like a prostitute, that is the picture in the language of verse seven. Without talk, she was just a used, old, other, "plain Jane". Gentlemen, you don't want your wife to feel used in any capacity. Jesus talked (and talks) to His bride all the time.

So far we have made it through two of these sensory components. Fasten your seatbelts for today we explore **taste**. By the way, I've especially chosen today to speak to this issue because while we are in a season of Lent, the best of the Lenten traditions have always excluded Sundays. Sundays are never for fasting; Sunday is a kingdom celebration, always and ever marked by feasting. The purple you see here today in our church is a seasonal reminder of Lent. We are not celebrating the Minnesota Vikings, the purple people eaters, but we are doing not only the next best thing, but also the very best thing as we remember the greater Solomon's feast. Psalm 34:8 says, "O, taste and see that the Lord is good". Song of Solomon 2:4 says, "He has brought us to a banqueting table and His banner over us is love". Love, marriage, banqueting, supper all go together all over the Bible; who could forget the Marriage supper of the Lamb. Love is always depicted as a banquet.

You know, I have long considered that the author of the book, "The Five Love Languages" really missed out here; they should be physical touch, affirming words, quality time, acts of service and gifts. Now perhaps you could say that food is in there somewhere, but if I were to write that book, FOOD would be more explicit.

I know some people whose love language is clearly food. Perhaps you remember the commercial over the holidays; I think the sponsor was Price Chopper, interviewing people about Holidays saying it's all about getting together with my crazy family and several other positive aspects to holidays. One guy pipes in, in a clear strong voice, a corrective tone, "It's all about the **food**".

Eating, drinking, and tasting are all over the Song of Solomon.[5] The Bible is filled with "eating metaphors" for loving, for taking something or someone into our inner most being. In Jeremiah 15:16 we read, "Thy words were found, and I did eat them, and Thy word was unto me the joy and rejoicing of my heart, for I am called by Thy name O Lord God of hosts".

Ezekiel ate the Word.
John in Revelation ate the Word.

When people talk about finding and experiencing something they love, they will say, "I ate it up"! It was wonderful, I found it, I couldn't get enough. Eating is also suggestive of the closet possible relationship. *Proverbs 4:17 "for they eat the bread of wickedness, and drink the wine of violence".* The bread is not a brand name like Roman Meal or Sunbeam. Wine is not like Yellow Tail or Manichevitz. Eating, drinking, and tasting are all parts of loving, literally and figuratively. For good or bad, the Bible does not shy away from this association. *Proverbs 30:20 " Such is the way of an adulterous woman; she eateth, and wipeth her mouth, and saith, I have done no wickedness"* and so the Song of Solomon is an exposition of this full sensory love relationship complete with tasting.

Let me mercifully delay getting into the detail of this by reminding us that this is not just about ancient history, nor is it a post-modern concept. Perhaps, you remember the block buster movie, "The Titanic". One of the characters was a woman named Rose, the movie opens, she is now very elderly, but back in 1912 the setting of the movie, she was in the flower of her youth. During a part of the

---

[5] This is as good a place as any to reference the influence and insight of James Jordan and Peter Leithart in the development of many of the major themes in this book.

movie, the elderly Rose is shown a provocative portrait of a young women from the recovered Titanic, and it turns out that it was her from way back then. There is then a scene in the movie where she is looking at the portrait and says something like; "If I don't say so myself, I was quite a dish". Now I assure you, she was not referring to whether or not the plate was paper, plastic, porcelain, or glass. She was referring to what was on the plate.

Solomon and His bride are likewise enjoying the feast. God help me and us all as we review some of this:

In the Song of Solomon we find:

Delights; 7:6 *"How fair and how pleasant art thou, O love, for delights"!*
Grapes; *Verse 7: "This thy stature is like to a palm tree, and thy breasts to clusters of grapes".*
Apples; *Verse 8: "I said, I will go up to the palm tree, I will take hold of the boughs thereof: now also thy breasts shall be as clusters of the vine, and the smell of thy nose like apples".*
Best of Wine; *Verse 9: "And the roof thy mouth like the best wine for my beloved, that goeth down sweetly, causing the lips of those that are asleep to speak".*
The vine, the grapes and the pomegranates; *Verse 12: "Let us get up early to the vineyards; let us see if the vine flourish, whether the tender grape appear, and the pomegranates bud forth, there will I give thee my love".*

Look at 6:2 & 3; *"My beloved is gone down into his garden, to the beds of spices, to feed in the gardens, and to gather lilies. I am my beloved's and my beloved is mine; he feedeth among the lilies".* **Yikes!**

Look at 2:16; *"My beloved is mine, and I am his: he feedeth among the lilies".*

Let's return to the text where we began. Song of Solomon 2:3-5; *"As the apple tree among the trees of the wood, so is my beloved among the sons. I sat down under his shadow with great delight, and his fruit was sweet to my taste. He brought me to the banqueting house, and his banner over me was love. Stay me with flagons, comfort me with apples; for I am sick of love".*

Talk about food as a love language! It has so much power to redeem and to reaffirm; sustain me, comfort me. We talk of comfort food literally, listen: there is no comfort food quite like love, and so we see this food and tasting, literally and figuratively here. Let us not forget, nor minimize, the power of food. There is a considerable truth to the old adage, the way to a man' heart is through his stomach. I will remember the earliest days of my relationship with Karen. Each night when I went home to my own place (and I did go home to my own place), she would make me a paper bag lunch for the next day; an act of service and food language combo. Remarkable impact, not only in calories, but presentation. When I grew up, there were boys, volumes, whole sandwiches, triple deckers, and wax paper. On the other hand, when I met Karen, she would slice my sandwich in half. I had never seen this before; sometimes diagonally in a neat little baggie. No longer was I spitting out wax, nor having it stuck between my teeth. Sometimes there was even an extra cookie or treat in my lunch.

God understands food and fasting, literally and figuratively. Our reading from John 6:48-51;

"I am the bread of life. Your fathers did eat manna in the wilderness, and are dead. This is the bread which cometh down from heaven, that a man may eat thereof and not die".

We partake of Him, how close are we to be to Him, and He to be to us. Our other reading Revelation 3:15 &

16; "*I know thy works, that thou art neither cold nor hot: I would thou wert cold or hot. So then because thou art lukewarm, and neither cold nor hot, I will spew thee out of my mouth*".

Wishing we were hot or cold, if not, He spits us out, He partakes of us.

In the next chapter we will be doing another component of the full sensory relationship, that of fragrance. By the way, did you know fragrance is related to what we eat? Try onions, garlic, or ginseng then ask someone what you smell like. By way of the communion table, we have the fragrance, the aroma of Jesus Christ.

Until then let us concentrate of Jesus, and let us consume together the feast given us by the lover of our soul, the greater Solomon, the Lord Jesus, and let us thereby be satisfied.

CHAPTER 5:
WHAT WILL YOU SEE IN THE SHULAMITE?

Song of Solomon 6:10-13b "Who is she that looketh forth as the morning, fair as the moon, clear as the sun, and terrible as an army with banners? I went down into the garden of nuts to see the fruits of the valley and to see whether the vine flourished, and the pomegranates budded. Or ever I was aware, my soul made me like the chariots of Amminadib. Return, return, O Shulamite; return, return, that we may look upon thee".

We will now turn our attention to sight! "What will you see in the Shulamite?" The Song of Solomon is filled with beautiful visual imagery. Solomon and his bride have the highest appreciation for the sheer physical and visual attractiveness of each other. They continually and correspondingly lavish praise upon praise for each other's beauty.

Song of Solomon 1:8 "If thou know not, O thou fairest among women, go thy way forth by the footsteps of the flock, and feed thy kids beside the shepherds' tents". Every part of each other's body and being is described in the fullness of its exquisite beauty.

Cheeks and the neck: *Song of Solomon 1:10 "Thy cheeks are comely with rows of jewels, thy neck with chains of gold".*

Song of Solomon 4:1;7 "Behold thou are fair, my love; behold, thou art fair; thou hast doves' eyes within thy locks, thy hair is as a flock of goats, that appear from mount Gilead. Thou art all fair, my love; there is no spot in thee."

Song of Solomon 4:9, 11 " Thou hast ravished my heart, my

sister, my spouse; thou hast ravished my heart with one of thine eyes, with one chain of thy neck. Thy lips, O my spouse, drop as the honeycomb; honey and milk are under thy tongue; and the smell of thy garments is like the smell of Lebanon."

Much of this gets far too detailed for this book. There is hair and teeth, thighs and hands, legs and belly buttons, and everything else you might imagine. The main point is in....

Song of Solomon 6:4,5, "Thou art beautiful, O my love, as Tirzah, comely as Jerusalem, terrible as an army with banners. Turn away thine eyes from me, for they have overcome me: thy hair is as a flock of goats that appear from Gilead."

(Of course, in 7:1 we see those shoes again. Guys cut her some slack on shoes.)

In chapter two, we have a sort of, as it were, Biblical version of Victoria's secret. Let's look at *Song of Solomon 2:14, "O my dove, that art in the clefts of the rock, in the secret places of the stairs, let me see thy countenance, let me hear thy voice, for sweet is thy voice and thy countenance is comely"*.

Surely these two are enjoying, delighting in seeing each other's beauty. God is not gnostic, neither should we be. Visual beauty plays a role, it matters, that is why we have pictures and mirrors. For good or ill, it played a role here. At the expense of calling him "shallow Solomon", let us look at *Song of Solomon 8:10, "I am a wall, and my breasts like towers, then was I in his eyes as one that found favor"*. Don't miss this significant point; beauty is in the eyes of the beholder, and here Solomon is the beholder. One of the several highlights of our Sweetheart Banquet was being entertained as we were reminded of that Old Love Song of a generation ago, "You are so beautiful to me".[6] Solomon viewed the Shulamite as beautiful, would we? Perhaps; perhaps she was an absolute knock out, perhaps not. In verse two of chapter seven, it says her belly was like a heap of wheat. The point is this, the Shulamite's not your wife or mine, for us it doesn't matter. For each other, beauty mattered, but for all the descriptive beauty complimented, there isn't a whole lot of …look at me, how beautiful I am. Remember *Proverbs 27:2 "Let another man praise thee, not your own mouth"*. As a matter of fact, there are indications that the Shulamite didn't view herself as "hot stuff" all that much.

"What will you see in the Shulamite?"

We may live in a generation where people are stuck on themselves, but that doesn't mean they were. Let me also be sure not to fail to provide a warning which is applicable to every generation, especially ours. Three times in the Song of Solomon we read this warning.

Song of Solomon 2:7 "I charge thee, O ye daughters of Jerusalem, by the roes, and by the hinds of the field, that ye stir not up, nor awake my love, till he please."

Song of Solomon 3:5 "I charge you, O ye daughters of Jerusalem, by the roes and by the hinds of the field, that ye stir not up, nor awake my love, till he please."

Song of Solomon 8:4 "I charge you, O daughters of Jerusalem, that ye stir not up, nor awake my love, until he please".

As we've taken a look at how important and powerful

---

[6] Sung so beautifully by the legendary Joe Cocker, most of whose songs make me want to "Cry Me A River".

visual stimulation can be, let us also take note of this ageless warning. There is a time for everything. Today we see young girls, kids, kindergarteners, dressed like street walkers, often encouraged by moms.

Now without nullifying or minimizing how "objectively" visually beautiful the Shulamite may or may not have been, remember beauty is in the eyes of the beholder. I now want to explore another aspect of beauty.

Look at *Song of Solomon 1:5-6 "I am black, but comely, O ye daughters of Jerusalem, as the tents of Kedar, as the curtains of Solomon. Look not upon me, because I am black, because the sun hath looked upon me; my mother's children were angry with me; they made me the keeper of the vineyards; but my own vineyard I have not kept."*

She did not want Solomon to see her, perhaps badly burned, but definitely a wreck. Her life consisted of taking care of everything but herself. There is here this picture of a sort of a Cinderella type, laboring in rags. This is a Talia Shire, an Adrian, from the Rocky movies, taking care of Paulie, and the pet shop.

You see, this other aspect of beauty that I don't think was lost on Solomon is the beauty of someone who is faithful and a worker, and loyal, and humble, and devoted and a servant. Perhaps he was not "shallow Solomon" after all. These traits are beautiful and very appealing. Here we have this book some might call racy and glossy, and yeah, she doesn't want to be seen when she's a wreck, but seven times her mother and Solomon's mother are invoked. Each time, with respect, honor, and high regard. Racy, glossy, self-absorbed people don't even think of their mothers, let alone speak well of them.

This beauty of devotion is very attractive and the

Shulamite had it. This is what we ought to see in the Shulamite. Beauty and devotion or loyalty goes together. Let me give some examples from the Bible.

How about Abigail? The Bible says explicitly she was beautiful; (1 Samuel 25:3). As beautiful as she was visually, she also was beautiful devotionally. She saved her husband's (Nabal = fool) life. She was devoted to him, to God, to David also, and spared him from committing murder. If you read all of chapter 25, you will see this. By the way, she also offers food, she is a servant; the way to a man's heart is through his stomach. The Bible says that the Lord smote Nabal and he died; afterward she became David's wife. In verse 41 of 1 Samuel 25 it says, *"Behold, let thine handmaid be a servant to wash the feet of the servants of my lord."* I remember my first Pastor commenting on this, he said if you find someone willing to wash your servant's feet, marry her.

How about Ruth? Ruth had this same devotional beauty; she was loyal to Naomi. *Ruth 1:16 & 17; "and Ruth said, entreat me not to leave thee, or to return from following after thee; for whither thou goest, I will go; and where thou lodgest, I will lodge; thy people shall be my people and thy God my God. Where thou diest, will I die, and there will I be buried; the Lord do so to me, and more also, if aught but death part thee and me."* Ruth was devotionally beautiful and she became Boaz's wife. *Ruth 2:11 & 12; "And Boaz answered and said unto her, it hath fully been shown me, all that thou hast done unto thy mother-in-law since the death of thine husband: and how thou has left thy father and thy mother, and the land of thy nativity, and art come unto a people which thou knewest not heretofore. The LORD recompense thy work, and a full reward be given thee of the LORD God of Israel, under whose wings thou art come to trust."* I don't think it is any surprise or mere coincidence (even though it was a sign) that Rebecca became Issac's wife, found by way of watering the donkeys.

Of course, you know that the Church is presented as a beautiful, glorious bride. Ezekiel 16 prefigures this in verse 1-14, and Ephesian 5:27 speaks of it. Revelation 19:7-8 shows a picture of her. The beauty is to be developed on a microcosmic and macrocosmic scale.

1 Peter 3:1-6, "Likewise, ye wives, be in subjection to your own husbands; that, if any obey not the word, they also may without the word be won by the conversation of the wives: while they behold your chaste conversation coupled with fear. Whose adorning let it not be that outward adorning of plaiting the hair, and of wearing of gold, or of putting on of apparel: but let it be the hidden man of the heart, in that which is not corruptible, even the ornament of a meek and quiet spirit, which is in the sight of God of great price. For after this manner in the old time the holy women also, who trusted in God adorned themselves being in subjection unto their own husbands: Even an Sarah obeyed Abraham, calling him lord: whose daughters you are, as long as you do well, and are not afraid with any amazement".

What will you see in the Shulamite?

I've given several examples of how beauty, devotional loyalty, and service go hand in hand. *Zechariah 11:7b, "and I took unto me two staves; the one I called beauty and the other I called Bands; and I fed the flock".* Here is an obscure prophecy that I remember teaching through several years ago. Graciousness and loyalty are universal bonds. When a society falls apart, it frays and things get ugly. That's another sermon for another time, but you get the idea, beauty and bands go together. Abigail was beautiful. Ruth was beautiful. Rebecca was beautiful. Sarah was beautiful. As the *Song of Solomon 6:13 says "What will you see in the Shulamite?"* She was devotionally and visually beautiful to Solomon. She found favor in his eyes.

I wonder how much you are willing to be like the

Shulamite? There is a challenge in this for us. Looking at *Song of Solomon 1:6* *"Look not upon me, because I am black, because the sun hath looked upon me: my mother's children were angry with me; they made me the keeper of the vineyards; but mine own vineyard have I not kept"*. Our mother is the Church, do we hold her in high regard? In thoughts and speech? And our mother's children are all of our brothers and sisters; are we loyal? Are we bound? Beauty goes with bonds. Are we devoted? Are we faithful? Are we servants? Are we willing to be slaves (in the good sense) to each other? Foot washing sort of stuff, like Abigail did for David's servants. Can we put others before ourselves or ahead of ourselves? Will we tend and keep their vineyards, at the expense and risk of ourselves, looking like we are a wreck? If we will, we may look like a wreck to the world, but Jesus, the greater Solomon; will sing, you are so beautiful to me! What will you see in the Shulamite? I hope you see yourself.

CHAPTER 6:
"SOLOMON'S OLD SPICE"

Song of Solomon 8:14; "Make haste, my beloved, and thou like to a roe or to a young hart upon the mountains of spices".

Fragrance is one of our five senses: sight, sound, touch, taste, and smell. The Song of Solomon depicts a full sensory love relationship. The Song of Solomon is the Holy of Holies, that place of full sensory fellowship, intimacy, even union with God.

Like the four other senses we have noted, the Song of Solomon does not fail to note the importance and power of smell. The very last word in the book is spices!

Back at the beginning of Advent, I spoke on making scents of Christmas; S C E N T S. Back then, I noted how, being the gnostic-prone Protestants we sometimes are, we often exclusively deal with making sense of Christmas at the expense of make scents of Christmas. When we do so, we display how much of an idol we have made our intellects.

The Song of Solomon by contrast, is not likened unto an S.A.T. test, an I.Q. test, or any other sort of testing of intelligence or intellectual aptitude.

When I was in college, I carried around with me a small tube of Coppertone sun/skin lotion. I'd open it from time to time just to get away. One whiff and I was transported to the beach complete with sunshine, ocean, and sand!

The Song of Solomon displays the power and importance of fragrance. I think I told you about the locker check we had last fall. One fabulous locker was instant aroma therapy: the glade made me glad.

It also can go the other way: our family van after transporting the boys soccer team! Remember *Ecclesiastes 10:1*... *"dead flies cause the ointment of the perfumer to send forth an evil odor".* Death stinks. Remember, that was a part of the fuss with Lazarus; *"Lord by this time he stinketh for he's been dead four days". John 11:39*

Just as I was taken away by just a whiff of Coppertone, so the lovers here are taken away with, they are enraptured by each other's fragrance. We will now work our way backwards through the story, making note of the **smells**.

Song of Solomon 7:13a "Thou dwellest in the gardens..."

7:8b, 9a "and the smell of thy nose like apples; and the roof of thy mouth like the best wine for my beloved..."

6:2 "My beloved is gone down into his garden, to the beds of spices, to feed in the gardens, and to gather lilies".

5:13 "His cheeks are as a bed of spices, as sweet flowers: his lips like lilies, dropping sweet smelling myrrh."

5:5 "I rose up to open to my beloved: and my hands dropped with myrrh and my fingers with sweet smelling myrrh upon the handlers of the lock".

5:1 "I am come into my garden, my sister, my spouse: I have gathered my myrrh with my spice; I have eaten my honeycomb with my honey: I have drunk my wine with my milk: eat O friends: drink, yeah, drink abundantly, O beloved".

4:13-16 "Thy plants are an orchard of pomegranates, with

pleasant fruits; camphire, with spikenard".

4:6 "Until the day break and the shadows flee away, I will get me to the mountain of myrrh and to the hill of frankincense".

4:10, 11 "How fair is thy love, my sister, my spouse! How much better is thy love than wine! And the smell of thine ointments than all spices! Thy lips, O my spouse, drop as the honeycomb: honey and milk are under thy tongue: and the smell of thy garments is like the smell of Lebanon".

3:6 "Who is this that cometh out of the wilderness like pillars of smoke, perfumed with myrrh and frankincense, with all powders of the merchant".

1:17 Irish spring! *"The beams of our house are cedar, and our rafters of fir".*

1:12-14 "While the king sitteth at his table, my spikenard sendeth forth the smell thereof. A bundle of myrrh is my well beloved unto me; he shall lie all night betwixt my breasts. My beloved is unto me as a cluster of camphire in the vineyards of En-gedi".

Notice the drawing power of fragrance.

1:3 & 4a "Because of the savour of thy good ointments thy name is as ointment poured forth, therefore do the virgins love thee. Draw me, we will run after thee".

One of the OCS Seniors wears a cologne he calls... "dark temptation". Whatever else we may think of that, it reminds us that fragrance has an alluring power and component. This alluring power and component is something that God understands and utilizes. As I mentioned during that advent sermon, the entire Bible is filled with references to the use of incense with God commending and sometimes even commanding it be so.

Aroma, perfume, fragrance, smell, odors, and incense are all over the Bible. They are not to be demonized and relegated to worldliness or worse. No where do you see God in His Word speaking against these things. With regard to incense: the context shows God angry with His people because they burn incense to other gods. It was not the burning of incense itself, it was giving to another that level of worship and devotion which belongs to Him alone! God was angry because Israel would go a whoring around and think that God was happy as long as she wore the perfume. Performance should match perfume. Of course, holiness does not come by wearing perfume, but holiness also does not come by not wearing perfume. When we demonize things like fragrance, we simply defer to the cults, and the occult to hijack them for their exclusive use.

Our constitution eviscerates dominion every time, and we are left to dwell in the squalor and stench of our own evangelical ghetto. As we've seen in the Song of Solomon, both bride and bridegroom are beautiful. We've read how both bride and bridegroom smell beautiful. There is a pleasant, attractive, alluring fragrance or aroma about each of them.

Certainly this is true of our bridegroom, The Lord Jesus.
Ps. 45:8 "All thy garments smell of myrrh and aloes."
Isaiah 60…prophecy, kings and camels, incense
Matthew 2   Kings, frankincense, myrrh and God

In life and death, he was perfumed.
John 12 spikenard, fragrance filled the house
John 19 body perfumed.
Luke 23 women came to the tomb to provide even more

What about a bride? Esther being prepped to be with

the king provides a clue.

Esther 2:12 "Now when every maid's turn was come to go in to king Ahasuerus, after that she had been twelve months, according to the manner of the women, (for so were the days of their purifications accomplished, to wit, six months with oil of myrrh, and six months with sweet odours, and with other things for the purifying of the women)".

More than that, St. Paul repeatedly speaks of us, that we are to be, and to have a sweet smelling savor.

Phil. 4:18 "But I have all, and abound: I am full, having received of Epaphroditus the things which were sent from you, an odour of a sweet smell, a sacrifice acceptable, well pleasing to God".

Ephesians 5:2 "And walk in love, as Christ also hath loved us, and hath given himself for us an offering and a sacrifice to God for a sweetsmelling savour".

2 Corinthians 2:14-16 "Now thanks be unto god, which always causeth us to triumph in Christ, and maketh manifest the savour of his knowledge by us in every place. For we are unto god a sweet savour of Christ, in them that are saved, and in them that perish: To the one we are the savour of death unto death; and to the other the savour of life unto life. And who is sufficient for these things?"

Worship... like the Song of Solomon. The Holy of Holies is reflective of the coming together of the bridegroom and his beloved. The Bible depicts this in its full sensory beauty. There is the commanding of incense in Exodus.

Exodus 30:1,8,"And thou shalt make an altar to burn incense upon: of shittim wood shalt thou make it. And when Aaron lighteth the lamps at even, he shall burn incense upon it, a perpetual incense before the LORD throughout your generations".

Exodus 30: 34-37 "And the LORD said unto Moses, take unto thee sweet spices, stacte, and onycha, and galbanum; these sweet spices with pure frankincense; of each shall there be a like weight: And thou shalt make it a perfume, a confection after the art of the apothecary, tempered together, pure and holy: And thou shall beat some of it very small and put of it before the testimony in the tabernacle of the congregation, where I will meet with thee: it shall be unto you most holy. And as for the perfume which thou shalt make, ye shall not make to yourselves according to the composition thereof, it shall be unto thee holy for the LORD".

Look at the anointing oil in Exodus 30:22-25 ingredient formulation. The Old Testament closes with this "worship" as perpetual in Malachi 1:11. We read from Revelation where we saw a worship ceremony in heaven. There we saw much incense. Whatever we may make of all this theologically and liturgically, let's be sure we bring it back to what it means for you and me.

I'll close with two points for your consideration, both of which struck a strong chord in me at the Tri-City, N.H. Conference.

First, we are reminded of worship, the way God likes it,[7] from Leviticus; the walk of worship, not ideology, a march, not a mood. How a person draws near is presented in the opening chapter of Leviticus. Those animal sacrifices representing us, ascend before God as a bride of pleasing aroma. Let us pause and consider; our walk through this worship pleases God, whereby we are not earning our salvation or any such things, but this

---

[7] In addition to the work of Jordan and Leithart, "The Lord's Service" by Jeff Meyers wonderfully develops the whys and wherefores of the Covenant Renewal Worship.

"having been drawn near" is pleasing. So on the one hand we are consumed by Him! He likes the way we smell!

Second, at the table, we partake of Him. Have you ever considered, we smell like what we eat. Eat onions; you will "ooze" onions. Karen eats ginseng candy, not unpleasant, but immediately detected.

Evangelicals often talk about the aroma of Christ or the fragrance of Christ, yet they rarely partake. We have the opportunity weekly to partake, of all people we ought to have the strongest and freshest fragrance of Christ.

Brothers and sisters, let us make the greater Solomon's Old Spice **our** old spice.[8]

---

[8] By the way, kudos to Joe Amedio for pointing out this notice on the Old Spice Deodorant container: "If your grandfather hadn't worn it, you wouldn't exist".

CHAPTER 7:
"I RAISED THEE UP"

Song of Solomon 8:5a "I raised thee up under the apple tree..."

We proclaim our faith, Jesus Christ is alive! He is risen from the dead! He is the first fruits of them that rise from the dead. This morning our focus is on the resurrection. Our God is the God who raised up Jesus. Our God is the God who raises us up. Our God is the God who raises the dead!

We begin our focus on the resurrection with the fact that resurrection comes in the context of death. Ephesians 2:1 says, "and you has he quickened (made alive) who were dead in trespasses and sins".

The Christian life and faith therefore, should not be viewed in a fashion so limited, so reduced, so truncated, as to merely proclaim that it is a "better life", or a more peaceful life, or a "more fulfilling life". As true as all of those are, the Christian faith is not merely an improved quality of life issue, it is a matter of life or death! Resurrection does not come in the context of life, resurrection comes in the context of death.

Jesus Christ was not merely awakened from a swoon or stupor. He was not merely revived. He did not merely morph into a higher plane of consciousness: Jesus Christ rose from the dead. Similarly, God meets us in the context of our death, and He raises us up. Our challenge thus is to think, act, and live more Biblically. As westerners, we tend to distinguish to the point of separation various events and treat them in isolation. On Good Friday, we study the cross. On Easter Sunday, we study the resurrection.

Brethren, distinguishing them to the point of separation, treating them in isolation, is to fail to see the power and the glory of God. The cross was never meant to be as a stand alone event; likewise, the resurrection, it was never mean to be as a standalone event.

Those of you familiar with Psalm 22 know this, a perfect picture, a prophesy of the cross, *Psalm 22:1-21 "my God, my God, why have you forsaken me"* and then in verse 22-31; a perfect picture of resurrection and the fruits thereof.

I say all this to serve as an introduction to one tiny clause in the Song of Solomon.

Song of Solomon 8:5a "I raised thee up under the apple tree.".

Here we see the works of God performed in "concert", resurrection taking place at the site of crucifixion. At the cross, beneath the cross of Jesus, so much life giving, resurrection work was being done, the next two clauses say "there".

There is where the Centurion said, "truly this was the Son of God". There is where Bunyan's Pilgrim had his burden lifted, and his sins rolled away. There at the cross the repentant thief heard these words, "today thou shalt be with me in paradise". There, the Church mothers many sons, who are fathered and born of God. There St. John huddled and embraced his new mother.

I know I'm spiritualizing and allegorizing this text. I'll do that even more in the weeks ahead when we use it to speak of our Mother, the church and then to thank God in giving honor to our earthly mothers.

Let us today, zoom out from the resurrection just enough so as to include the life giving work under the tree.

It is in the context of death that resurrection comes. In the Song of Solomon we read:

Song of Solomon 8:5a "I raised thee up under the apple tree".

Many of you have translations that say... awakened; "to open the eyes". The cross of Jesus Christ was and is a real eye opener; eyes indeed are opened at the cross. Remember Isaiah's prophecy of the cross? It really begins in chapter 52:13-15.

Isaiah 52:13-15 "Behold, my servant shall deal prudently, he shall be exalted and extolled, and be very high. As many were astonished at thee; his visage was so marred more than any man, and his form more than the sons of men: So shall he sprinkle many nations; the kings shall shut their mouths at him: for that which had not been told them shall they see; and that which they had not heard shall they consider".

The "spectacle" of the cross was startling and astounding! The cross: a real eye opener! The cross of Jesus Christ has opened more eyes than any other event in history. Maybe today, you will be awakened. Maybe today, you will be raised up! Maybe today of you it will be said, "I raised thee up under the apple tree".

In a bit, we are going to talk a little more about that "apple" tree, that "apple" aspect, but first note three things. Firstly, this tree is the best of trees.

Song of Solomon 2:3 "As the apple tree among the trees of the wood, so is my beloved among the sons."

Jesus is the greatest of all mankind. Secondly, trees in the Bible depict so much; the tree of life is found from Genesis to Revelation and is always known for its life giving fruit. In Genesis, Adam said, "I could have had the tree of life". The tree of life represents life itself in:

Revelation 22:1 – 2. "And HE showed me a pure river of water of life, clear as crystal, proceeding out of the throne of God and of the Lamb. In the midst of the street of it, and on either side of the river, was there the tree of life, which bare twelve manner of fruits, and yielded her fruit every month: and the leaves of the tree were for the healing of the nations".

Proverbs 11:30 "The fruit of the righteous is a tree of life; and he that winneth souls is wise".

Proverbs 13:12 "Hope deferred maketh the heart sick: but when the desire cometh, it is a tree of life".

Other trees in the Bible refer to peace, rest and community, as well as life. The fig tree in the Bible is all about times when God grants those sort of blessing, peace, rest community. (1 Kings 4:25; Micah 4:4; Zechariah 3:10). Of course, in the New Testament, Jesus calls Nathaniel from under the fig tree, (John 1:50).

Thirdly, trees are significant. For to be hung on a tree is a special disgrace.

Deuteronomy 21:23 "His body shall not remain all night upon the tree, but thou shalt in any wise bury him that day; (for he that is hanged is accursed of God;) that thy land be not defiled, which the LORD thy god giveth thee for an inheritance".

Galatians 3:13 "Christ hath redeemed us from the curse of the law, being made a curse for us: for it is written, cursed is everyone that hangeth on a tree".

Our Lord Jesus Christ is seen in all of these. He is the best. He is the tree of life, peace, rest, and community. He was accused, disgraced in our place.

All of this alone is startling, eye opening enough and yet there is more. The characterization of this as an apple tree adds even greater significance. Let's look again at the Song of Solomon 8:5:

Song of Solomon 8:5a "I raised thee up under the apple tree".

The word translated "apple", literally speaks of fruit, but even more directly and poignantly to fragrance. Some translations even call this as taking place beneath the "apricot tree". The Hebrew word points to a "fruity fragrance". In the last chapter we saw fragrance all thru the Song of Solomon: "Solomon's Old Spice". We concluded that chapter with how we as living sacrifices are to have the fragrance of Jesus Christ.

The cross of Jesus Christ was and is a life giving, sweet smelling, sacrificial aroma which has risen up, and has satisfied the God of Justice! Therefore He says ~ "I raised thee up under the apple tree." God's satisfaction with and at the cross remains the basis for our hope of resurrection. This is not about apples, nothing in the world, in all of history was as beautifully fragrant, spiritually as the cross of Jesus Christ.

At our Good Friday service, our program cited the word "passion" at several points. The "passion" of our Lord. In our modern day usage, people speak of passion all the time, something they like; something they are excited about; something that makes them happy. We kick that word around: I have a passion for ice-cream. The older understanding of the word has a significantly different connotation. How's this for some word association: passion = endure, agony, suffering, harm, destruction. The passion of Jesus Christ was a sweet smelling sacrifice offering unto God. However grotesquely ugly it was, at the same time it was spiritually beautiful. The hymn writer of the "Old Rugged Cross" said that it had a wondrous attraction. He said that he saw a wondrous beauty there; sacrificial suffering is beautiful. The Roman church "beautifies", declares a saint, those like Mother Teresa who live beautifully sacrificial lives.

Maybe you are into sports; a wonderful picture of passion, sacrifice, suffering. NBA city, a restaurant in Universal studios, contains a full size depiction of Dennis Rodman diving for a loose ball. There is nothing beautiful about Dennis Rodman. He is completely horizontal, some four feet off the ground. The end of which is hurt, pain; passion/suffering, sacrifice, the offering of one's body.

Dedication and devotion are wonderfully attractive and wondrously beautiful traits. They are inspiring, they raise us up! I'm not sure who Josh Groban is singing about when He sings you raise me up. Have you ever heard this song? You raise me up, to stand on mountains, to walk on stormy seas, I am strong when I am on your shoulders, you raise me up to more than I can be. I'm not sure who he is singing about. I do know that only Jesus Christ can do all that and more. However else inspiring anyone else can be, only Jesus Christ, only God can raise us from the dead.

No Mother Teresa, Dennis Rodman, Tony Robbins, no Mohammed can inspire to the point of raising the dead. This markedly separates the Christian faith as superior to all other faiths.

I would like to close this chapter with a poem, perhaps you are familiar with it. It links the cross to our hope of resurrection. It is from the book "When Hell was in Session" by Jeremiah Denton, about his experience as a prisoner of war for nearly eight years in North Vietnam.

"The soldiers stare, then drift away. Young John finds nothing he can say. The veil is rent, the deed is done, and Mary holds her only son. His limbs grow stiff, the night grows cold, but naught can loose that mother's hold. Her gentle anguished eyes seem blind, who knows what thoughts run thru her mind. Perhaps she thinks of last week's palms with cheering thousands offering alms, or dreams of Cana on that day, she nagged him until she got her way. Her face shows grief, but not despair, her head though bowed has faith to spare. For even now she could suppose his thorns might somehow yield a rose. Her life with him was full of signs that God writes straight with crooked lines: Dark clouds can hide the rising sun, and all seem lost, when all be won!"

Your life may be filled with darkness and suffering now; do not despair. That is precisely the context when God brings new life. Jesus' resurrection and ours in mere revival, no mere increase of interest, or inspiration, no mere improvement in the quality of our lives! Resurrection only comes in the context of death. Therefore God says: "I raised thee up under the apple tree!"

CHAPTER 8:
"OUR ALMA MATER"

Song of Solomon 8:5 "Who is this that cometh up from the wilderness, leaning upon her beloved? I raised thee up under the apple tree: there thy mother brought thee forth: there she brought thee forth that bare thee."

Our Alma Mater: Alma Mater is Latin for "nurturing mother". The Alma Mater I am going to talk about is not where you went to High School or College; not OCS, CCHS, Troy High, Tamarac or Lansingburgh or Siena. The Alma Mater I am going to talk about is the Church of Jesus Christ. She is our Alma Mater, she is our nurturing mother, and she has no graduates save those who have left this life graduating on to their eternal reward and rest.

We might call this nurturing mother our "other mother", and we do well to make note today that Mother's day is a mere two weeks from today. Some of us men need that sort of heads-up. Public Service announcement: Mother's Day is in two weeks. Come Mother's Day, Lord willing, we will talk about our earthly moms, but today let's talk about our other nurturing mother, our Alma Mater, the Church of the Lord Jesus Christ.

What a glorious and beautiful picture the Bible gives us of our Alma Mater. You know, it is amazing to me that in so many sectors, the Church is roundly and universally despised, dishonored, and disrespected and not only amongst pagans and those of the world; but even among those claiming to be believers! How often we hear: "Jesus yes; Church no".

This is all the more so remarkably sad and tragic because the Bible, the "ought to be" source book for believers, so roundly and uniformly shows tremendous honor and respect to the Church, our Alma Mater; the bride of our Lord Jesus! In Ephesians 5:26 & 27 we read about how Jesus is sanctifying, washing, cleansing her, to the end that she becomes a glorious Church without spot or wrinkle. Modern day men and women may very well despise her, but that is not at all how God views her, or how men and women of old viewed her.

Today we will explore all of that, as well as our text in the Song of Solomon 8:5.

Song of Solomon 8:5 "Who is this that cometh up from the wilderness, leaning upon her beloved? I raised thee up under the apple tree: there thy mother brought thee forth: there she brought thee forth that bare thee."

Previously we read, "I raised thee up under the apple tree". In that passage we saw the sacrificial satisfying fragrance of Jesus offering of himself in our place. We noted how "beneath the cross of Jesus" so many great and wonderful things took place. The foot of the cross of Jesus Christ is that greatest "eye opening" site and event in all of history. There God sprinkled and startled many nations. There is where we are raised up! There is where awakening takes place! There is where new life is brought forth! There under the cross we see our Alma Mater.

Look at the following clauses; there thy mother brought thee forth, there she brought thee forth who bore thee. Brethren this is a wonderful picture of the work of the Church. This is a wonderful picture of our nurturing mother, our Alma Mater.

You know, we're not talking today about Oakwood, or St. Stephens, or 1st Presbyterian, or Third Baptist, or any other particular or localized body. We are talking about the Church. We are talking about the God-ordained entity God has raised up, through whom all who are His children come forth. All of you here who claim the Name of Jesus, who claim to be a Christian, you have a mother, you have an Alma Mater! Remember what St. Paul said:

Galatians 4:26 "But Jerusalem which is above is free, which is the mother of us all."

He cites this same mechanism to describe his own work.

Galatians 4:19 "My little children, of whom I travail in birth again until Christ be formed in you".

All of you, each of you, came to Christ in some fashion by way of the Church. However minimal it may have seemed, someone witnessed, someone left a tract. The monks left us the copied scriptures; our grandmothers sung us the songs. All these and a thousand other things have been the work of the church. All who come, come through her!

I was reminded of this several times this last week at our recent dinner theater, "American Ideal". OCS Senior Mark Fisher, playing the role of Brother Jackson, speaking to Simon Coward on Saturday night, (students tend to go little more off script the second night) during one exchange said "Simon my man, my brother, "my home-slice". I asked Mark this week what he meant by "my home-slice". He said, you know, "we're tight". I responded, I need more, then he said, "you know, my brother from another mother". "My brother from another mother", of course I know what that means. It has become a common way for Christians to refer to each other, (same God, different biological mother); the problem is, it isn't true. All Christians have one father and one mother. All Christians have the same father and the same mother. God is not a polygamist. All Christians have the same Alma Mater.

How does God speak about this mother? Psalm 87 describes her well.

Psalm 87:1-7 "His foundation is the holy mountains, the Lord loveth the gates of Zion more than all the dwellings of Jacob. Glorious things are spoken of thee, O city of God. Selah. I will make mention of Raham and Babylon to them that know me: behold Philistia, and Tyre, with Ethiopia; this man was born there. And of Zion it shall be said, this and that man was born in her; and the highest himself shall establish her. The LORD shall count, when he writeth up the people, that this man was born there. Selah. As well the singers as the players on instruments shall be there: all my springs are in thee."

Zion, the spiritual city of God, she is our nurturing mother. What a picture of God's zeal for His glorious bride. How about Isaiah 62.

Vs. 1: For Zion's sake
Vs. 2: For Jeremiah's sake

God would not rest or hold his peace until she abided in glorious fullness.

Vs. 2 Glory
Vs. 3 Royal diadem
Vs. 4 Not forsake or desolate – don't diss her
But my delight is in her" Heph – zibah and "Married" – Beulah.

Vs. 5 God rejoices over her
Vs. 6 Watchmen are set….

58

Vs. 7 and are not supposed to rest till Jerusalem is a praise in all the earth. We have a long way to go; our work is cut out for us. Christians ought not be diminishing that which God wants developing.

Zion is this nurturing mother. Look at Isaiah 66. Mary was a type of this (verse 7-9), giving birth, and the Church is the fulfillment (verse 10-14). What a picture, this nurturing mother, this Alma Mater. It's the same picture in the Song of Solomon.

*Song of Solomon 8:1-2 "O That thou wert as my brother, that sucked the breasts of my mother! When I should find thee without, I would kiss thee; yea I should not be despised. I would lead thee, and bring thee into **my mother's house**, who would instruct me: I would cause thee to drink of spiced wine of the juice of my pomegranate."*

My mother's house; my mother's house is the Father's house. God and His bride are not as dysfunctional as we are. News flash: In a Biblical Church, mom and dad, (bride and groom), live together and the kids should come home. The individual bride here in Song of Solomon, the Shulamite, she understands the value of her mother. That same value was not lost on the Saints of old. How important is she? St. Augustine said, "you cannot have God as Father without the Church as Mother". From the Reformers: (to whom we owe our Protestant heritage), responding even in the midst of ecclesiastical abuses, even they spoke highly of her and of her indispensible role.

Martin Luther, (not the Pope), the pioneer of Protestantism said, "apart from the Church salvation is impossible". Listen to John Calvin: (not exactly a Roman Catholic sympathizer), "The Church is the mother, and she has the milk and the food that the Father has provided to nourish his adopted children". He concludes: "This is why the Church is called the mother of believers. And certainly, he who refuses to be a son of the Church desires in vain to have God as his Father." In another place he said this, "Let us learn even from the simple title "mother" how useful, indeed how necessary, it is that we should know the church. For there is no other way to enter life unless this mother conceive us in her womb, give us birth, nourish us at her breast, and lastly, unless she keep us under her care and guidance until putting off mortal flesh we become like the angels. Our weakness does not allow us to be dismissed from her school until we have been pupils all our lives. Furthermore, away from her bosom one cannot hope for any forgiveness of sins or salvation."

This Church, this nurturing mother, has been around for a long time, and she will abide even into eternity. She's not perfect yet, and her pilgrimage has been marked by hardship. Our nurturing mother has always known the wilderness, and she knows the way out. She's been there, and done that!

Acts 7:38 "This is he, that was in the church in the wilderness with the angel which spake to him in the mount Sina, and with our fathers: who received the lively oracles to give unto us".

Revelation 12:1-6 "And there appeared a great wonder in heaven; a woman clothed with the sun, and the moon under her feet, and upon her head a crown of twelve stars: and she being with child cried, travailing in birth, and pained to be delivered. And there appeared another wonder in heaven; and behold a great red dragon, having seven heads and ten horns, and seven crowns upon his heads. And his tail drew the third part of the stars of heaven and did cast them to the earth: and the dragon stood before the woman which was ready to be delivered, for to devour her child as soon as it was born. And the woman fled into the wilderness, where she hath a place prepared of God, that they should feed her there a thousand two hundred and threescore days".

This life giving, nurturing mother has been through trial, tribulation, and wilderness. Our Alma Mater knows the wilderness and the way out.

Song of Solomon 8:5-6a "Who is this that cometh up from the wilderness, leaning upon her beloved? I raised thee up under the apple tree: there thy mother brought thee forth: there she brought thee forth that bare thee. Set me as a seal upon thine heart, as a seal upon thine arm."

Leaning, just as the Priests of Leviticus would lean on those animal sacrificial offerings, so she, so we, the Church of Jesus Christ lean on Him. So strong is the bond we are to have with Jesus Christ, that we read in verse six, set me as a seal upon thine heart. For sure, this nurturing mother is not to move; in thought, word, or deed even one inch from her beloved. There and there alone in His arms does she abide safely.

As we begin to wind down here, there are many things that mothers do: shop, cook, clean, instruct, and provide nurture of every sort. The Church is no different, providing all sorts of activities; activities that can be lawfully engaged in, and Biblically encouraged; there's a time and place for all of them. All of these are glorious acts of nurturing.

Jesus gives us a picture of this kingdom work in Luke.

Luke 13:18-19 "Then said he, unto what is the kingdom of God like? And whereunto shall I resemble it? It is like a grain of mustard seed, which a man took, and cast into his garden; and it grew, and waxed a great tree, and the fowls of the air lodged in the branches of it."

Our Alma Mater has done all this sort of stuff and

more; she's been responsible for: schools, hospitals, red cross, orphanages, shelters, clinics, etc. Nurturing is what alma means, but what principally defines a mother? It is that she gives birth, she brings forth life, and so here at Oakwood our central focus, our central concentration must remain to abide beneath the cross of Jesus, for it is there, there under the tree we give birth, and we become our Alma Mater.

CHAPTER 9:
"HIS MOTHER CROWNED HIM"

Song of Solomon 3:11 "Go forth, O ye daughters of Zion, and behold king Solomon with the crown wherewith his mother crowned him in the day of his espousals, and in the day of the gladness of his heart."

Happy Mother's Day to all of you moms out there, we are going to speak about mothers, as the Song of Solomon does.

I've mentioned in our series from this book that mothers are referenced here, in fact, seven times in the Song. In each and every case it is in the context of respect, support, and appreciation. In the last chapter we noted the Church as our Alma Mater, our nurturing mother.

Our theme for this chapter is to note, as the Bible does, the role of women in the lives of their children. We will use the specific example of Bathsheba, Solomon's mother, as well as some other examples from the Bible and history to help us draw conclusions and applications about whom and what moms are, and about how we are to honor them. We do well today to remember the commandment, honor thy father and thy mother! Let's all recite that out loud together. "Honor thy father and thy mother".

Here in the Song of Solomon, this erotic romance novel, we see this seeming station break like commentary from an unknown voice saying..."*Go forth, O ye daughters of Zion, and behold King Solomon with the crown wherewith his mother crowned him*". The main focus here is King Solomon, Behold, and look at him! The crown is in the picture for sure, that crown helped beautify him, and so is his mom,

63

somewhere here in the background. Isn't that just as it is, and as it should be? The focus of a mom's life is pouring herself into her children. For a mother, it's not "all about me", it's all about them.

It was the day of His espousals; it was the day of the gladness of his heart. She was not the main attraction, she wasn't trying to steal the show, but she was "there"; there in every good and proper sense, present, supporting, preparing, supplying, and investing.

Moms are sometimes behind the scenes. Moms may or may not be in the picture at all, but they are always pulling for, plugging for, crowing, and cheering on their children. By and large, what any of us become, we owe to our mothers and to those who have mothered us! This includes moms of every sort, spiritual and/or biological, who rejoice in the prosperity of their children.

Remember *3 John 2 -4 "Beloved, I wish above all things that thou mayest prosper and be in health, even as thy soul prospereth. For I rejoiced greatly, when the brethren came and testified of the truth that is in thee, even as thou walkest in the truth. I have no greater joy than to hear that my children walk in truth".*

Mothers, both spiritual and biological, rejoice in the advance and blessing of their children. As good as all that is, the picture that I'm painting for you here, and as we will see in the Bible, is not limited to mom merely being some sort of cheerleader, or some sideliner, or emotional support person, though she is that; she is so much more. There was some research done in conjunction with the US Bureau of Labor statics: mom's worth is at least $507,000 per year. She is an animal caretaker, an executive chef, a computer systems analyst, financial manager, food and beverage service worker, general office clerk, a registered nurse, a management analyst, a childcare worker, a housekeeper, a psychologist, a bus driver, an elementary school principal, a dietitian and nutritionist, a property manager, a social worker and a recreation worker, just to name a few. But that's not nearly all; there are some things that money just can't buy. As Karol Ladd writes in her book, "the Power of a Positive Mom", some things are "priceless" including the following: kissing a boo-boo, fixing a favorite meal, making birthdays special, getting up during the night for feedings or illnesses, adjudicating sibling disputes, scratching backs, baking warm cookies, telling stories at bedtime, holding hands, giving a hug, a smile, a word of encouragement.

In our school we had a contest this week, in part to make an acronym of Mom – "M O M"; one elementary student summed it up perfectly: "MANAGER OF ME".

But moms are more than just managers, listen to this from Thomas Edison, the great inventor.

"I did not have my mother long, but she cast over me an influence which has lasted all my life. The good effects of her early training I can never lose. If it had not been for her appreciation and her faith in me at a critical time in my experience, I should never likely have become an inventor. I was always a careless boy, and with a mother of different caliber, I should have turned out badly. But her firmness, her sweetness, her goodness were potent powers to keep me in the right path. My mother was the making of me."

My mother was the making of me, not just the manager of me, the making of me. Before we go back to the Bible and Bathsheba and Solomon, let me encourage two fabulous resources.[9] One: "Recovering Biblical

---

[9] Each of these books, as well as (the later mentioned) Kelly Corrigan's "The Middle Place" contain anecdotal and statistical information highlighting the significance of family,

Manhood and Womanhood", a 1993 book of the year. When Napoleon asked what could be done to restore the nation, his reply was bold and blunt, "give us better mothers". Two: This sort of book is not my normal cup of tea, but perhaps because it's revised and updated, "The Power of a Positive Mom". Mom's influence is beyond measure. Some chapters include: apples of gold, the power and importance of words, great expectations, study your kids, see their potential, and offer opportunities for growth, set goals, support their endeavors. In another chapter, the beauty of a smile, we read about Frederic Batholdi who was the sculptor for the Statue of Liberty, and how he chose his own mother's image as the face of lady liberty because she was the most heroic and influential person in his life!

Let's get back to the Bible and Bathsheba, Solomon's mother and this business of the crown. Please note when we read of this crown in chapter three of the Song of Solomon, please note this shouldn't be confused with his coronation as King, but interestingly, she was there in that as well. David was old and stricken in years and about to lose the kingdom to Adonijah. You can read all about this in the opening thirty-seven verses of 1 Kings 1.

The crown Solomon wore as King over Israel in large part got there by Bathsheba. The crown, Solomon wore at his wedding in the Song of Solomon was placed there by Bathsheba as well. Never underestimate the power and influence of a mother. I was reminded of this last week as I was watching the news. Surfing thru, being sure to be able to successfully avoid Brian Williams, I landed on another network and the story of Kelly Corrigan. Did you see this? Kelly Corrigan has this wildly successful book

---

particularly mothers.

"The Middle Place" of which her own mother said, "it was so-so, we are not rich or poor". What she meant is that there was nothing special about them. She wondered how can this book sell, when they were not famous, and there was nothing spectacular to note. Yet, that same mother went on a crusade visiting book stores, and promoting it. She moved the books to more prominent shelves and locations. She would approach, cold call, and talk with total strangers, have you read this? Try this, you'll really like it. In large part, through all that pulling and plugging, Mama Corrigan made quite a crown for Kelly.

Of course these things can be overdone. In Matthew 20:20-21, the mother of Zebedee's children comes and asks Jesus if her sons can sit on his right and his left hand in His kingdom. This is a mother's version of "the kingdom of God suffers violence and the violent take it by force".

What kind of crown did Bathsheba crown Solomon with? This was a wedding wreath type of crown; it remains a part of Jewish and Eastern Orthodox tradition to note the coronation aspect of the husband as king and the wife as queen during the wedding ceremony. But this crown has an array of flowers and jewels. Again, she is participating in the fullest for his big day, participating in his joy and in the gladness, participating in the beautification of her son and of the event.

Weddings in Biblical times, unlike today where there is almost exclusive attention to the bride, highlighted the groom as the centerpiece. The parallels and parables of the bridegroom's processional reveals this focus. That whole galaxy of things we associate with prepping a bride, were then on Solomon the groom.

Now I've not had occasion to be a mother or take on

that whole galaxy of things we associate with prepping a bride, but I know someone going through that right now, Norma. Right Norma? I say this with great respect. Norma is into this wedding: the particulars, details, beauty, attention, notice. There is no question, but that her heart and head and hands are into this. A mother cannot but be into the day of their child's espousal, the day of gladness of their heart.

I walked in on a conversation between her and my wife, Karen about centerpieces. I don't know if they were for reception, rehearsal dinner, or shower, but the conversation was all about whether or not those centerpieces would rightly bring out the colors in the tablecloths! They wouldn't say it in these terms but they were concerned about the spectrum analysis of the refractive of angles at which the light would be reflected off the contours of the centerpieces. Before I was married, I didn't even know or care what a tablecloth was! For me, it worked for wiping your hands. But see for Norma and Bathsheba, no detail is too small, no decision too inconsequential! "There is meaning in the minutia". Mothers make "crowns" for their children's day of espousals; mothers make "crowns" for the day of the gladness of their hearts. Norma's doing a great job; every indication is that Bathsheba did as well. Norma, don't think too hard on this, but your daughter expects to marry one man, Solomon had 700 wives. His mother, Bathsheba was probably known to mumble under breath, after 700, thank God for concubines!! There were 300 of those.

There are two other points I want to make as I close this chapter. The crown was noteworthy. The commentators focused on Solomon, but did not fail to mention the crown. It was a good crown.

Secondly, and related to this, don't miss "he wore it".

She honored him by making it, by placing it, and he honored her by wearing it. There was none of this, him saying, "this is goofy or stupid or embarrassing". Rather, "He wore it"; sounds like it could be a whole other sermon.

I'll close where we began, "honor your father and your mother". And you know, there are no term limits to their office or this commandment. Bathsheba was probably fairly old when she made and placed this crown. We, as others in every culture and era have a tendency to despise old age, but Proverbs 23:22 says, *"Hearken unto thy father that begot thee and despise not thy mother when she is old"*.

Solomon's mother crowned him, and he wore it.

Go and do likewise.

CHAPTER 10:
"GRACE TO RUN"

Song of Solomon 1:4 A "Draw me, after thee.... We will run".

Grace to Run. This morning we are going to explore how love impacts lives. Love brings energy, passion, power, excitement, motivation. Love brings life.

The old King James word sums it up powerfully, "Love Quickens". Today we are going to talk about love. This applies to human love, man and wife. That is what Song of Solomon is all about.

This applies also to love of country. On this Memorial Day weekend, we should note how love of country brings motivation. Our heritage, (our memorializing of fallen and sacrificing fellow countrymen) is a source of quickening for us.

But supremely, because His love is supreme, this applies to whom God is and what He has done for us. His love quickens, empowers. His love makes us run! Draw me after thee, we will run.

Today we are going to explore this link and relationship of love to this quickening, and it should be applied across at least all three of these areas:

Human love – person to person - quickens

Love of country - quickens

Love of God - quickens

You know, we often talk about the race to run. The duties of our lives, the paths we take, the course we pursue

71

and yes we have a race to run. Today it's not so much about the race to run, today is more foundational than that, today is about us being the recipients of grace - grace to run.

The end result of those who are loved, the end result of those who have received this grace, the end result is not questionable. The end result is definitive; We Will Run. "Draw me after thee....We will Run"!

The love story of the Song of Solomon begins and ends with this energizing theme not only here in chapter one but glance over to the last verse of chapter eight. "Make haste... upon the mountains", from beginning to end, this book is all about Love! What a picture, skipping across the mountains, love, bringing energy, passion, power, excitement, motivation. Love brings Life! Love quickens. You and I have a race to run, and God who is love gives us grace to run.

Before we delve into the detail of this, I do want to note that this sermon is closing out our series on the Song of Solomon. This is our 10th sermon of the series; few people in history have done more than a handful. For those of you who think that I've already talked about this way too much, let me remind you that the Song, as the veritable "Holy of Holies" really is inexhaustible: for if there is one thing that has no limit – it is love.

"Song of Solomon 8:7 Many waters cannot quench love, neither can the floods drown it; if a man would give all the substance of his house for love, it would utterly be contemned."

In the 12th century, Bernard of Clairvaux began preaching through the Song. He preached 86 sermons and only got to the end of chapter two, stopping there because he died. His disciple Gilbert Porretanus preached another

48 sermons, made it to Chapter 5:10, when he died. Remember, few others have done more than a handful. I figure that if I count St. Bernard's 86 and add Porretanus 48, that makes for 134, tacking on my 10 makes for 144. A good clean, round, Biblical number referencing and symbolizing fullness, completeness, and vastness. One hundred forty-four is a good place to stop, for love is limitless.

You know, running is a wonderful picture of life and love, and we see it all over the Bible. Even good human relationships are a source of and cause for zeal, excitement, enthusiasm for running. In Luke 15:20 (when the prodigal son was still a great way off on his way home), his father saw him and ran, fell on his neck and kissed him. If this is true on the human level, and it is, (it is what the Song is all about) how much more between you and God!! The fact that God energizes, the testimony that God provides grace to run is all over the Bible.

Let's turn to *1 Kings 18:46 "And the hand of the LORD was on Elijah; and he girded up his loins, and ran before Ahab to the entrance of Jezreel".* By the hand of God, he ran a veritable marathon.

Let's look at a couple of Psalms:

Psalm 18:20 "For by thee I have run through a troop; and by my God have I leaped over a wall."

"By thee" when God acts in our lives, wild horses can't stop us.

Psalm 63:7 & 8 "Because thou hast been my help, therefore in the shadow of thy wings will I rejoice, my soul followeth hard after thee: thy right hand upholdeth me."

My soul follows hard after thee. This "following hard" is sandwiched by God's grace; you have been my help, your right hand upholds me.

Psalm 119:32 "I will run the way of thy commandments, when thou shalt enlarge my heart".

In our own strength we can't walk the way of His commandments, we have no power, zeal, or drive. In John 15:5, Jesus says, without me, apart from me, you can do nothing, not a little bit of something. In Psalm 119, without Him enlarging my heart, I cannot run. Without Christ we are all like the Grinch, hearts several sizes too small. In Christ, we have a race to run, and He gives grace to run.

The Bible speaks frankly of our fallen condition:

Isaiah 40:28-31"Hast thou not known? Hast thou not heard, that the everlasting God, the LORD, the Creator of the ends of the earth, fainteth not, neither is weary? There is no searching of his understanding".

Proverbs 18:14 "The spirit of a man will sustain him in his infirmity but a wounded spirit who can bear"?

I've been there and done that. Our fallen condition is so great that Jesus says, no man can come to me unless the Father draws him.

Proverbs 13:12 "Hope deferred maketh the heart sick, but when the desire cometh, it is a tree of life".

Do you remember how St. Peter opens his Epistle?

1 Peter 1:3 "Blessed be the God and Father of our Lord Jesus Christ, which according to his abundant mercy hath begotten us again unto a lively hope by the resurrection of Jesus Christ from the dead".

"...A lively hope, by the resurrection...". The ancient origin of the word hope is to hop, to leap, to bounce, to "jump for joy".

The people of God are begotten again; they are born again unto a lively hope. The resurrection has consequences; it is not an abstract, dry, sterile doctrine. It has consequences; it has legs, even literally. It puts a hope in our hearts. It puts a hop in our step. The boss, Bruce Springsteen talks about tramps like us being born to run from the law. The Bible talks about us being saints, born again to run to God and for God.

Do you know that Zaccheus ran ahead to meet Jesus.? Even the rich, young ruler ran out to meet Jesus. Years ago, I preached on how run is a great contraction for resurrection. Both words begin with R. Both words end with N. both words contain the vowel "U" in the middle. When "U" are right in the middle of that word and "U" are right in the middle of God's plan, His plan is for "U" to run, to run with those, and as those, who ran on Resurrection morning.

"Run" is a great contraction of Re**s**U**rrectio**N: Look what they did.

*John 20:1-4 "The first day of the week cometh Mary Magdalene early, when it was yet dark unto the sepulcher, and seeth the stone taken away from the sepulcher. Then she **runneth**, and cometh to Simon Peter, and to the other disciple, whom Jesus loved, and saith unto them, they have taken away the Lord out of the sepulcher, and we know not where they have laid him. Peter therefore went forth and that other disciple, and came to the sepulcher, so they **ran** both together; and the other disciple did **outrun** Peter, and came first to the sepulcher".*

*Luke 24:12 "Then arose Peter, and **ran** unto the sepulcher; and stooping down, he behold the linen clothes laid by themselves, and departed wondering in himself at that which was come to pass".*

*Matthew 28:6-8 "He is not here; for he is risen, as he said. Come, see the place where the Lord lay and **go quickly**, and tell his disciples that he is risen from the dead; and behold he goeth before you into Gailiee; there shall ye see him; lo, I have told you. And they **departed quickly** from the sepulcher with fear and great joy; and did **run** to bring his disciples word".*

In Mark's account, (16:8) it is written that the disciples fled (another form of running).

Faith runs. Unbelief sits – note 2 Kings 7:3ff.

Did you know that one act of zeal saved a continent?

Acts 8:26-30 "And the angel of the Lord spake unto Philip, saying, Arise, and go toward the south unto the way that goeth down from Jerusalem unto Gaza, which is desert. And he arose and went, and behold a man of Ethiopia, an eunuch of great authority under Candace queen of the Ethiopians who had the charge of all her treasure, and had come to Jerusalem for to worship, was returning and sitting in his chariot read Esaias the prophet. Then the Spirit said unto Philip, go near, and join thyself to this chariot. And Philip ran thither to him, and hear him read the prophet Esaias and said, understandest thou what thou readest?"

You know, I have scripture after scripture about running, zeal, and urgency. All associated with the work of God. Habbakuk, and Zechariah talk about folks running, flocking to Him. In our reading from Isaiah 55, we learn of our invitation to run to Him.

Isaiah 55:1-5 "Ho every one that thirsteth, come ye to the waters, and he that hath no money; come ye, buy and eat, yea come,

76

*buy wine and milk without money and without price. Wherefore do
ye spend money for that which is not bread? And your labour for that
which satisfieth not? Hearken diligently unto me and eat ye that
which is good and let your soul delight itself in fatness. Incline your
ear and come unto me, hear and your soul shall live, and I will make
an everlasting covenant with you, even the sure mercies of David.
Behold I have given him for a witness to the people, a leader and
commander to the people. Behold thou shalt call a nation that thou
knowest not, and nations that knew not thee shall run unto thee
because of the LORD thy God and for the Holy one of Israel, for he
hath glorified thee.*

The Old Testament closes with a picture:

*Malachi 4:2 "But unto you that fear my name shall the Sun of
righteousness arise with healing in his wings and ye shall go forth,
and grow up as calves of the stall".*

You don't see the word "run" here, but you do see
"go forth". I see this at home, did you know we have a
baby bull? I open that barn door, out comes exuberance,
energy, zeal, liberation! The son of righteousness does the
same in us.

Song of Solomon 1:4A "Draw me, after thee…. We will run".

When he draws us, we not only can run, we will run.
When God's hand and spirit are upon you, you will run.
We not only have a race to run, we've been given the grace
to run.

The Song of Solomon, the Song of Songs, the best of
songs shows us this life-giving grace. We know that
love, as good as it is, that which happens between man
and wife, is but a picture of what happens between Christ
and His bride. It's been said,

77

"God's commands have become His enabling's...

> To run and work the law commands;
> yet gives me neither feet nor hands;
> but better news the gospel brings,
> it bids me fly and gives me wings". [10]

Draw me after thee.   We will run!

---

[10] See "The Epistle of Paul to the Romans" by F.F. Bruce in the Tyndale New Testament Commentary Series, p.162.

www.ingramcontent.com/pod-product-compliance
Lightning Source LLC
Chambersburg PA
CBHW071833020426
42331CB00007B/1716